The Intellectuals and Socialism

F.A. Hayek

I

IN ALL DEMOCRATIC countries, in the United States even more than elsewhere, a strong belief prevails that the influence of the intellectuals on politics is negligible. This is no doubt true of the power of intellectuals to make their peculiar opinions of the moment influence decisions, of the extent to which they can sway the popular vote on questions on which they differ from the current views of the masses. Yet over somewhat longer periods they have probably never exercised so great an influence as they do today in those countries. This power they wield by shaping public opinion.

In the light of recent history it is somewhat curious that this decisive power of the professional second-hand dealers in ideas should not yet be more generally recognised. The political development of the Western world during the last hundred years furnishes the clearest demonstration. Socialism has never and nowhere been at first a working-class movement. It is by no means an obvious remedy for the obvious evil which the interests of that class will necessarily demand. It is a construction of theorists, deriving from certain tendencies of abstract thought with which for a long time only the intellectuals were familiar; and it required long efforts by the intellectuals before the working classes could be persuaded to adopt it as their programme.

In every country that has moved toward socialism, the phase of the development in which socialism becomes a determining influence on politics has been preceded for many years by a period during which socialist ideals governed the thinking of the more active intellectuals. In Germany this stage had been reached towards the end of the last century; in England and France, about the time of the First World War. To the casual observer it would seem as if the United States had reached this phase after World War II and that the attraction of a planned and directed economic system is now as strong among the American intellectuals as it ever was among their German or English fellows. Experience suggests that, once this phase has been reached, it is merely a question of time until the views now held by the intellectuals become the governing force of politics.

9

The character of the process by which the views of the intellectuals influence the politics of tomorrow is therefore of much more than academic interest. Whether we merely wish to foresee or attempt to influence the course of events, it is a factor of much greater importance than is generally understood. What to the contemporary observer appears as the battle of conflicting interests has indeed often been decided long before in a clash of ideas confined to narrow circles. Paradoxically enough, however, in general the parties of the Left have done most to spread the belief that it was the numerical strength of the opposing material interests which decided political issues, whereas in practice these same parties have regularly and successfully acted as if they understood the key position of the intellectuals. Whether by design or driven by the force of circumstances, they have always directed their main effort towards gaining the support of this 'élite', while the more conservative groups have acted, as regularly but unsuccessfully, on a more naïve view of mass democracy and have usually vainly tried directly to reach and to persuade the individual voter.

II

The term 'intellectuals', however, does not at once convey a true picture of the large class to which we refer, and the fact that we have no better name by which to describe what we have called the second-hand dealers in ideas is not the least of the reasons why their power is not better understood. Even persons who use the word 'intellectual' mainly as a term of abuse are still inclined to withhold it from many who undoubtedly perform that characteristic function. This is neither that of the original thinker nor that of the scholar or expert in a particular field of thought. The typical intellectual need be neither: he need not possess special knowledge of anything in particular, nor need he even be particularly intelligent, to perform his role as intermediary in the spreading of ideas. What qualifies him for his job is the wide range of subjects on which he can readily talk and write, and a position or habits through which he becomes acquainted with new ideas sooner than those to whom he addresses himself.

Until one begins to list all the professions and activities which belong to this class, it is difficult to realise how numerous it is, how the scope for its activities constantly increases in modern society, and how dependent on it we all have become. The class does not consist only of journalists, teachers, ministers, lecturers, publicists, radio commentators, writers of fiction, cartoonists, and artists—all of whom may be masters of the technique of conveying ideas but are usually amateurs so far as the substance of what they convey is concerned. The class also includes many professional men and technicians, such as scientists and doctors, who through their habitual intercourse with the printed word become carriers of new ideas outside their own fields and who, because of their expert knowledge of their own subjects, are listened to with respect on most others. There is little that the ordinary man of today learns about events or ideas except through the medium of this class; and outside our special fields of work we are in this respect almost all ordinary men, dependent for our information and instruction on those who make it their job to keep abreast of opinion. It is the intellectuals in this sense who decide what views and opinions are to reach us, which facts are important enough to be told to us, and in what form and from what angle they are to be presented. Whether we shall ever learn of the results of the work of the expert and the original thinker depends mainly on their decision.

The layman, perhaps, is not fully aware to what extent even the popular reputations of scientists and scholars are made by that class and are inevitably affected by its views on subjects which have little to do with the merits of the real achievements. And it is specially significant for our problem that every scholar can probably name several instances from his field of men who have undeservedly achieved a popular reputation as great scientists solely because they hold what the intellectuals regard as 'progressive' political views; but I have yet to come across a single instance where such a scientific pseudo-reputation has been bestowed for political reason on a scholar of more conservative leanings. This creation of reputations by the intellectuals is particularly important in the fields where the results of expert studies are not used by other specialists but depend on the political decision of the public at large. There is indeed scarcely a better illustration of this than the attitude which professional economists have taken to the growth of such doctrines as socialism or protectionism. There was probably at no time a majority of economists, who were recognised as such by their peers, favourable to socialism (or, for that matter, to protection).

In all probability it is even true to say that no other similar group of students contains so high a proportion of its members decidedly opposed to socialism (or protection). This is the more significant as in recent times it is as likely as not that it was an early interest in socialist schemes for reform which led a man to choose economics for his profession. Yet it is not the predominant views of the experts but the views of a minority, mostly of rather doubtful standing in their profession, which are taken up and spread by the intellectuals.

The all-pervasive influence of the intellectuals in contemporary society is still further strengthened by the growing importance of 'organisation'. It is a common but probably mistaken belief that the increase of organisation increases the influence of the expert or specialist. This may be true of the expert administrator and organiser, if there are such people, but hardly of the expert in any particular field of knowledge. It is rather the person whose general knowledge is supposed to qualify him to appreciate expert testimony, and to judge between the experts from different fields, whose power is enhanced. The point which is important for us, however, is that the scholar who becomes a university president, the scientist who takes charge of an institute or foundation, the scholar who becomes an editor or the active promoter of an organisation serving a particular cause, all rapidly cease to be scholars or experts and become intellectuals in our sense, people who judge all issues not by their specific merits but, in the characteristic manner of intellectuals, solely in the light of certain fashionable general ideas. The number of such institutions which breed intellectuals and increase their number and powers grows every day. Almost all the 'experts' in the mere technique of getting knowledge over are, with respect to the subject matter which they handle, intellectuals and not experts.

In the sense in which we are using the term, the intellectuals are in fact a fairly new phenomenon of history. Though nobody will regret that education has ceased to be a privilege of the propertied classes, the fact that the propertied classes are no longer the best educated and the fact that the large number of people who owe their position solely to their general education do not possess that experience of the working of the economic system which the administration of property gives, are important for understanding the role of the intellectual. Professor Schumpeter, who has devoted an illuminating chapter of his *Capitalism,*

Socialism, and Democracy to some aspects of our problem, has not unfairly stressed that it is the absence of direct responsibility for practical affairs and the consequent absence of first-hand knowledge of them which distinguishes the typical intellectual from other people who also wield the power of the spoken and written word. It would lead too far, however, to examine here further the development of this class and the curious claim which has recently been advanced by one of its theorists that it was the only one whose views were not decidedly influenced by its own economic interests. One of the important points that would have to be examined in such a discussion would be how far the growth of this class has been artificially stimulated by the law of copyright.[1]

III

It is not surprising that the real scholar or expert and the practical man of affairs often feel contemptuous about the intellectual, are disinclined to recognise his power, and are resentful when they discover it. Individually they find the intellectuals mostly to be people who understand nothing in particular especially well and whose judgement on matters they themselves understand shows little sign of special wisdom. But it would be a fatal mistake to underestimate their power for this reason. Even though their knowledge may be often superficial and their intelligence limited, this does not alter the fact that it is their judgement which mainly determines the views on which society will act in the not too distant future. It is no exaggeration to say that, once the more active part of the intellectuals has been converted to a set of beliefs, the process by which these become generally accepted is almost automatic and irresistible. These intellectuals are the organs which modern society has developed for spreading knowledge and ideas, and it is their convictions and opinions which operate as the sieve through which all new conceptions must pass before they can reach the masses.

It is of the nature of the intellectual's job that he must use his own knowledge and convictions in performing his daily task. He occupies his position because he possesses, or has had to deal from day to day with, knowledge which his employer in general does not possess, and his activities can therefore be directed by others only to a limited extent. And just because the intellectuals are mostly intellectually honest, it is inevitable that they should follow their own convictions whenever they have discretion and that they should give a corresponding slant to everything that passes through their hands. Even where the direction of policy is in the hands of men of affairs of different views, the execution of policy will in general be in the hands of intellectuals, and it is frequently the decision on the detail which determines the net effect. We find this illustrated in almost all fields of contemporary society. Newspapers in 'capitalist' ownership, universities presided over by 'reactionary' governing bodies, broadcasting systems owned by conservative governments, have all been known to influence public opinion in the direction of socialism, because this was the conviction of the personnel. This has often happened not only in spite of, but perhaps even because of, the attempts of those at the top to control opinion and to impose principles of orthodoxy.

The effect of this filtering of ideas through the convictions of a class which is constitutionally disposed to certain views is by no means confined to the masses. Outside his special field the expert is generally no less dependent on this class and scarcely less influenced by their selection. The result of this is that today in most parts of the Western world even the most determined opponents of socialism derive from socialist sources their knowledge on most subjects on which they have no first-hand information. With many of the more general preconceptions of socialist thought, the connection of their more practical propos-als is by no means at once obvious; in consequence, many men who believe themselves to be determined opponents of that system of thought become in fact effective spreaders of its ideas. Who does not know the practical man who in his own field denounces socialism as 'pernicious rot' but, when he steps outside his subject, spouts socialism like any Left journalist?

In no other field has the predominant influence of the socialist intellectuals been felt more strongly during the last hundred years than in the contacts between different national civilis-ations. It would go far beyond the limits of this article to trace the causes and significance of the highly important fact that in the modern world the intellectuals provide almost the only approach to an international community. It is this which mainly accounts for the extraordinary spectacle that for generations the suppos-edly 'capitalist' West has been lending its moral and material support almost exclusively to those ideological movements in the countries farther east which aimed at undermining Western civilisation and that, at the same time, the information which the Western public has obtained about events in Central and Eastern Europe has almost inevitably been coloured by a socialist bias. Many of the 'educational' activities of the American forces of occupation in Germany have furnished clear and recent examples of this tendency.

IV

A proper understanding of the reasons which tend to incline so many of the intellectuals towards socialism is thus most important. The first point here which those who do not share this bias ought to face frankly is that it is neither selfish interests nor evil intentions but mostly honest convictions and good intentions which determine the intellectuals' views. In fact, it is necessary to recognise that on the whole the typical intellectual is today more likely to be a socialist the more he is guided by good will and intelligence, and that on the plane of purely intellectual argument he will generally be able to make out a better case than the majority of his opponents within his class. If we still think him wrong, we must recognise that it may be genuine error which leads the well-meaning and intelligent people who occupy those key positions in our society to spread views which to us appear a threat to our civilisation.[2] Nothing could be more important than to try to understand the sources of this error in order that we should be able to counter it. Yet those who are generally regarded as the representatives of the existing order and who believe that they comprehend the dangers of socialism are usually very far from such understanding. They tend to regard the socialist intellectuals as nothing more than a pernicious bunch of highbrow radicals without appreciating their influence and, by their whole attitude to them, tend to drive them even further into opposition to the existing order.

If we are to understand this peculiar bias of a large section of the intellectuals, we must be clear about two points. The first is that they generally judge all particular issues exclusively in the light of certain general ideas; the second, that the characteristic errors of any age are frequently derived from some genuine new truths it has discovered, and they are erroneous applications of new generalisations which have proved their value in other fields.

The conclusion to which we shall be led by a full consideration of these facts will be that the effective refutation of such errors will frequently require further intellectual advance, and often advance on points which are very abstract and may seem very remote from the practical issues.

It is perhaps the most characteristic feature of the intellectual that he judges new ideas not by their specific merits but by the readiness with which they fit into his general conceptions, into the picture of the world which he regards as modern or advanced. It is through their influence on him and on his choice of opinions on particular issues that the power of ideas for good and evil grows in proportion to their generality, abstractness, and even vagueness. As he knows little about the particular issues, his criterion must be consistency with his other views and suitability for combining into a coherent picture of the world. Yet this selection from the multitude of new ideas presenting themselves at every moment creates the characteristic climate of opinion, the dominant *Weltanschauung* of a period, which will be favourable to the reception of some opinions and unfavourable to others and which will make the intellectual readily accept one conclusion and reject another without a real understanding of the issues.

In some respects the intellectual is indeed closer to the philosopher than to any specialist, and the philosopher is in more than one sense a sort of prince among the intellectuals. Although his influence is farther removed from practical affairs and correspondingly slower and more difficult to trace than that of the ordinary intellectual, it is of the same kind and in the long run even more powerful than that of the latter. It is the same endeavour towards a synthesis, pursued more methodically, the same judgement of particular views in so far as they fit into a general system of thought rather than by their specific merits, the same striving after a consistent world view, which for both forms the main basis for accepting or rejecting ideas. For this reason the philosopher has probably a greater influence over the intellectuals than any other scholar or scientist and, more than anyone else, determines the manner in which the intellectuals exercise their censorship function. The popular influence of the scientific specialist begins to rival that of the philosopher only when he ceases to be a specialist and commences to philosophise about the progress of his subject—and usually only after he has

been taken up by the intellectuals for reasons which have little
to do with his scientific eminence.

The 'climate of opinion' of any period is thus essentially a set of
very general preconceptions by which the intellectual judges the
importance of new facts and opinions. These preconceptions are
mainly applications to what seem to him the most significant
aspects of scientific achievements, a transfer to other fields of
what has particularly impressed him in the work of the specialists. One could give a long list of such intellectual fashions and
catchwords which in the course of two or three generations have
in turn dominated the thinking of the intellectuals. Whether it
was the 'historical approach' or the theory of evolution, nineteenth century determinism and the belief in the predominant
influence of environment as against heredity, the theory of
relativity or the belief in the power of the unconscious—every one
of these general conceptions has been made the touchstone by
which innovations in different fields have been tested. It seems
as if the less specific or precise (or the less understood) these
ideas are, the wider may be their influence. Sometimes it is no
more than a vague impression rarely put into words which thus
wields a profound influence. Such beliefs as that deliberate
control or conscious organisation is also in social affairs always
superior to the results of spontaneous processes which are not
directed by a human mind, or that any order based on a plan
laid down beforehand must be better than one formed by the
balancing of opposing forces, have in this way profoundly
affected political development.

Only apparently different is the role of the intellectuals where
the development of more properly social ideas is concerned. Here
their peculiar propensities manifest themselves in making
shibboleths of abstractions, in rationalising and carrying to
extremes certain ambitions which spring from the normal
intercourse of men. Since democracy is a good thing, the further
the democratic principle can be carried, the better it appears to
them. The most powerful of these general ideas which have
shaped political development in recent times is of course the
ideal of material equality. It is, characteristically, not one of the
spontaneously grown moral convictions, first applied in the
relations between particular individuals, but an intellectual
construction originally conceived in the abstract and of doubtful
meaning or application in particular instances. Nevertheless, it

has operated strongly as a principle of selection among the alternative courses of social policy, exercising a persistent pressure towards an arrangement of social affairs which nobody clearly conceives. That a particular measure tends to bring about greater equality has come to be regarded as so strong a recommendation that little else will be considered. Since on each particular issue it is this one aspect on which those who guide opinion have a definite conviction, equality has determined social change even more strongly than its advocates intended.

Not only moral ideals act in this manner, however. Sometimes the attitudes of the intellectuals towards the problems of social order may be the consequence of advances in purely scientific knowledge, and it is in these instances that their erroneous views on particular issues may for a time seem to have all the prestige of the latest scientific achievements behind them. It is not in itself surprising that a genuine advance of knowledge should in this manner become on occasion a source of new error. If no false conclusions followed from new generalisations, they would be final truths which would never need revision. Although as a rule such a new generalisation will merely share the false consequences which can be drawn from it with the views which were held before, and thus not lead to new error, it is quite likely that a new theory, just as its value is shown by the valid new conclusions to which it leads, will produce other new conclusions which further advance will show to have been erroneous. But in such an instance a false belief will appear with all the prestige of the latest scientific knowledge supporting it. Although in the particular field to which this belief applies all the scientific evidence may be against it, it will nevertheless, before the tribunal of the intellectuals and in the light of the ideas which govern their thinking, be selected as the view which is best in accord with the spirit of the time. The specialists who will thus achieve public fame and wide influence will thus not be those who have gained recognition by their peers but will often be men whom the other experts regard as cranks, amateurs, or even frauds, but who in the eyes of the general public nevertheless become the best known exponents of their subject.

In particular, there can be little doubt that the manner in which during the last hundred years man has learned to organise the forces of nature has contributed a great deal towards the creation of the belief that a similar control of the forces of society would bring comparable improvements in human conditions. That, with the application of engineering techniques, the direction of all forms of human activity according to a single coherent plan should prove to be as successful in society as it has been in innumerable engineering tasks, is too plausible a conclusion not to seduce most of those who are elated by the achievement of the natural sciences. It must indeed be admitted both that it would require powerful arguments to counter the strong presumption in favour of such a conclusion and that these arguments have not yet been adequately stated. It is not sufficient to point out the defects of particular proposals based on this kind of reasoning. The argument will not lose its force until it has been conclusively shown why what has proved so eminently successful in producing advances in so many fields should have limits to its usefulness and become positively harmful if extended beyond these limits. This is a task which has not yet been satisfactorily performed and which will have to be achieved before this particular impulse towards socialism can be removed.

This, of course, is only one of many instances where further intellectual advance is needed if the harmful ideas at present current are to be refuted and where the course which we shall travel will ultimately be decided by the discussion of very abstract issues. It is not enough for the man of affairs to be sure, from his intimate knowledge of a particular field, that the theories of socialism which are derived from more general ideas will prove impracticable. He may be perfectly right, and yet his resistance will be overwhelmed and all the sorry consequences which he foresees will follow if he is not supported by an effective refutation of the *idées mères*. So long as the intellectual gets the better of the general argument, the most valid objections to the specific issue will be brushed aside.

V

This is not the whole story, however. The forces which influence recruitment to the ranks of the intellectuals operate in the same direction and help to explain why so many of the most able among them lean towards socialism. There are of course as many differences of opinion among intellectuals as among other groups of people; but it seems to be true that it is on the whole the more active, intelligent, and original men among the intellectuals who most frequently incline towards socialism, while its opponents are often of an inferior calibre. This is true particularly during the early stages of the infiltration of socialist ideas; later, although outside intellectual circles it may still be an act of courage to profess socialist convictions, the pressure of opinion among intellectuals will often be so strongly in favour of socialism that it requires more strength and independence for a man to resist it than to join in what his fellows regard as modern views. Nobody, for instance, who is familiar with large numbers of university faculties (and from this point of view the majority of university teachers probably have to be classed as intellectuals rather than as experts) can remain oblivious to the fact that the most brilliant and successful teachers are today more likely than not to be socialists, while those who hold more conservative political views are as frequently mediocrities. This is of course by itself an important factor leading the younger generation into the socialist camp.

The socialist will, of course, see in this merely a proof that the more intelligent person is today bound to become a socialist. But this is far from being the necessary or even the most likely explanation. The main reason for this state of affairs is probably that, for the exceptionally able man who accepts the present order of society, a multitude of other avenues to influence and power are open, while to the disaffected and dissatisfied an intellectual career is the most promising path to both influence and the power to contribute to the achievement of his ideals. Even more than that: the more conservatively inclined man of first class ability will in general choose intellectual work (and the sacrifice in material reward which this choice usually entails) only if he enjoys it for its own sake. He is in consequence more likely to become an expert scholar rather than an intellectual in the specific sense of the word; while to the more radically minded the intellectual pursuit is more often than not a means rather than an end, a path to exactly that kind of wide influence which the professional intellectual exercises. It is therefore probably the fact, not that the more intelligent people are generally socialists, but that a much higher proportion of socialists among the best minds devote themselves to those intellectual pursuits which in modern society give them a decisive influence on public opinion.[3]

The selection of the personnel of the intellectuals is also closely connected with the predominant interest which they show in general and abstract ideas. Speculations about the possible entire reconstruction of society give the intellectual a fare much more to his taste than the more practical and short-run considerations of those who aim at a piecemeal improvement of the existing order. In particular, socialist thought owes its appeal to the young largely to its visionary character; the very courage to indulge in Utopian thought is in this respect a source of strength to the socialists which traditional liberalism sadly lacks. This difference operates in favour of socialism, not only because speculation about general principles provides an opportunity for the play of the imagination of those who are unencumbered by much knowledge of the facts of present-day life, but also because it satisfies a legitimate desire for the understanding of the rational basis of any social order and gives scope for the exercise of that constructive urge for which liberalism, after it had won its great victories, left few outlets. The intellectual, by his whole disposition, is uninterested in technical details or practical difficulties. What appeal to him are the broad visions, the specious comprehension of the social order as a whole which a planned system promises.

This fact that the tastes of the intellectual were better satisfied by the speculations of the socialists proved fatal to the influence of the liberal tradition. Once the basic demands of the liberal programmes seemed satisfied, the liberal thinkers turned to problems of detail and tended to neglect the development of the general philosophy of liberalism, which in consequence ceased to be a live issue offering scope for general speculation. Thus for something over half a century it has been only the socialists who have offered anything like an explicit programme of social development, a picture of the future society at which they were aiming, and a set of general principles to guide decisions on particular issues. Even though, if I am right, their ideals suffer from inherent contradictions, and any attempt to put them into practice must produce something utterly different from what they expect, this does not alter the fact that their programme for change is the only one which has actually influenced the development of social institutions. It is because theirs has become the only explicit general philosophy of social policy held by a large group, the only system or theory which raises new problems and opens new horizons, that they have succeeded in inspiring the imagination of the intellectuals.

The actual developments of society during this period were determined not by a battle of conflicting ideals, but by the contrast between an existing state of affairs and that one ideal of a possible future society which the socialists alone held up before the public. Very few of the other programmes which offered themselves provided genuine alternatives. Most of them were mere compromises or half-way houses between the more extreme types of socialism and the existing order. All that was needed to make almost any socialist proposal appear reasonable to these 'judicious' minds who were constitutionally convinced that the truth must always lie in the middle between the extremes, was for someone to advocate a sufficiently more extreme proposal. There seemed to exist only one direction in which we could move, and the only question seemed to be how fast and how far the movement should proceed.

VI

The significance of the special appeal to the intellectuals which socialism derives from its speculative character will become clearer if we further contrast the position of the socialist theorist with that of his counterpart who is a liberal in the old sense of the word. This comparison will also lead us to whatever lesson we can draw from an adequate appreciation of the intellectual forces which are undermining the foundations of a free society.

Paradoxically enough, one of the main handicaps which deprives the liberal thinker of popular influence is closely connected with the fact that, until socialism has actually arrived, he has more opportunity of directly influencing decisions on current policy and that in consequence he is not only not tempted into that long-run speculation which is the strength of the socialists, but is actually discouraged from it because any effort of this kind is likely to reduce the immediate good he can do. Whatever power he has to influence practical decisions he owes to his standing with the representatives of the existing order, and this standing he would endanger if he devoted himself to the kind of speculation which would appeal to the intellectuals and which through them could influence developments over longer periods. In order to carry weight with the powers that be, he has to be 'practical', 'sensible', and 'realistic'. So long as he concerns himself with immediate issues, he is rewarded with influence, material success, and popularity with those who up to a point share his general outlook. But these men have little respect for those speculations on general principles which shape the intellectual climate. Indeed, if he seriously indulges in such long-run speculation, he is apt to acquire the reputation of being 'unsound' or even half a socialist, because he is unwilling to identify the existing order with the free system at which he aims.[4]

If, in spite of this, his efforts continue in the direction of general speculation, he soon discovers that it is unsafe to associate too closely with those who seem to share most of his convictions, and he is soon driven into isolation. Indeed there can be few more thankless tasks at present than the essential one of developing the philosophical foundation on which the further development of a free society must be based. Since the man who undertakes it must accept much of the framework of the existing order, he will appear to many of the more speculatively minded intellectuals merely as a timid apologist of things as they are; at the same time he will be dismissed by the men of affairs as an impractical theorist. He is not radical enough for those who know only the world where 'with ease together dwell the thoughts' and much too radical for those who see only how 'hard in space together clash the things'. If he takes advantage of such support as he can get from the men of affairs, he will almost certainly discredit himself with those on whom he depends for the spreading of his ideas. At the same time he will need most carefully to avoid anything resembling extravagance or over-statement. While no socialist theorist has ever been known to discredit himself with his fellows even by the silliest of proposals, the old-fashioned liberal will damn himself by an impracticable suggestion. Yet for the intellectuals he will still not be speculative or adventurous enough, and the changes and improvements in the social structure he will have to offer will seem limited in comparison with what their less restrained imagination conceives.

At least in a society in which the main requisites of freedom have already been won and further improvements must concern points of comparative detail, the liberal programme can have none of the glamour of a new invention. The appreciation of the improvements it has to offer requires more knowledge of the working of the existing society than the average intellectual possesses. The discussion of these improvements must proceed on a more practical level than that of the more revolutionary programmes, thus giving a complexion which has little appeal for the intellectual and tending to bring in elements to whom he feels directly antagonistic. Those who are most familiar with the working of the present society are also usually interested in the preservation of particular features of that society which may not be defensible on general principles. Unlike the person who looks for an entirely new future order and who naturally turns for guidance to the theorist, the men who believe in the existing order also usually think that they understand it much better than any theorist and in consequence are likely to reject whatever is unfamiliar and theoretical.

The difficulty of finding genuine and disinterested support for a systematic policy for freedom is not new. In a passage of which the reception of a recent book of mine has often reminded me, Lord Acton long ago described how:

> at all times sincere friends of freedom have been rare, and its triumphs have been due to minorities, that have prevailed by associating themselves with auxiliaries whose objects differed from their own; and this association, which is always dangerous, has been sometimes disastrous, by giving to opponents just grounds of opposition...[5]

More recently, one of the most distinguished living American economists has complained in a similar vein that the main task of those who believe in the basic principles of the capitalist system must frequently be to defend this system against the capitalists—indeed the great liberal economists, from Adam Smith to the present, have always known this.

The most serious obstacle which separates the practical men who have the cause of freedom genuinely at heart from those forces which in the realm of ideas decide the course of development is their deep distrust of theoretical speculation and their tendency to orthodoxy; this, more than anything else, creates an almost impassable barrier between them and those intellectuals who are devoted to the same cause and whose assistance is indispensable if the cause is to prevail. Although this tendency is perhaps natural among men who defend a system because it has justified itself in practice, and to whom its intellectual justification seems immaterial, it is fatal to its survival because it deprives it of the support it most needs. Orthodoxy of any kind, any pretence that a system of ideas is final and must be unquestioningly accepted as a whole, is the one view which of necessity antagonises all intellectuals, whatever their views on particular issues. Any system which judges men by the completeness of their conformity to a fixed set of opinions, by their 'soundness' or the extent to which they can be relied upon to hold approved views on all points, deprives itself of a support without which no set of ideas can maintain its influence in modern society. The ability to criticise accepted views, to explore new vistas and to experiment with new conceptions, provides the atmosphere without which the intellectual cannot breathe. A cause which offers no scope for these traits can have no support from him and is thereby doomed in any society which, like ours, rests on his services.

VII

It may be that a free society as we have known it carries in itself the forces of its own destruction, that once freedom has been achieved it is taken for granted and ceases to be valued, and that the free growth of ideas which is the essence of a free society will bring about the destruction of the foundations on which it depends. There can be little doubt that in countries like the United States the ideal of freedom has today less real appeal for the young than it has in countries where they have learned what its loss means. On the other hand, there is every sign that in Germany and elsewhere, to the young men who have never known a free society, the task of constructing one can become as exciting and fascinating as any socialist scheme which has appeared during the last hundred years. It is an extraordinary fact, though one which many visitors have experienced, that in speaking to German students about the principles of a liberal society one finds a more responsive and even enthusiastic audience than one can hope to find in any of the Western democracies. In Britain also there is already appearing among the young a new interest in the principles of true liberalism which certainly did not exist a few years ago.

Does this mean that freedom is valued only when it is lost, that the world must everywhere go through a dark phase of socialist totalitarianism before the forces of freedom can gather strength anew? It may be so, but I hope it need not be. Yet, so long as the people who over longer periods determine public opinion continue to be attracted by the ideals of socialism, the trend will continue. If we are to avoid such a development, we must be able to offer a new liberal programme which appeals to the imagination. We must make the building of a free society once more an intellectual adventure, a deed of courage. What we lack is a liberal Utopia, a programme which seems neither a mere defence of things as they are nor a diluted kind of socialism, but a truly liberal radicalism which does not spare the susceptibilities of the mighty (including the trade unions), which is not too severely practical, and which does not confine itself to what appears today as politically possible. We need intellectual leaders who are prepared to resist the blandishments of power and influence and who are willing to work for an ideal, however small may be the prospects of its early realisation. They must be men who are willing to stick to principles and to fight for their full realisation, however remote. The practical compromises they must leave to the politicians. Free trade and freedom of opportunity are ideals which still may arouse the imaginations of large numbers, but a mere 'reasonable freedom of trade' or a mere 'relaxation of controls' is neither intellectually respectable nor likely to inspire any enthusiasm.

The main lesson which the true liberal must learn from the success of the socialists is that it was their courage to be Utopian which gained them the support of the intellectuals and therefore an influence on public opinion which is daily making possible what only recently seemed utterly remote. Those who have concerned themselves exclusively with what seemed practicable in the existing state of opinion have constantly found that even this has rapidly become politically impossible as the result of changes in a public opinion which they have done nothing to guide. Unless we can make the philosophic foundations of a free society once more a living intellectual issue, and its implementation a task which challenges the ingenuity and imagination of our liveliest minds, the prospects of freedom are indeed dark. But if we can regain that belief in the power of ideas which was the mark of liberalism at its best, the battle is not lost. The intellectual revival of liberalism is already under way in many parts of the world. Will it be in time?

Printed in the USA
CPSIA information can be obtained
at www.ICGtesting.com
LVHW071635020224
770787LV00003B/378

9 781169 830493

The Long Waves In Economic Life

Nikolai D. Kondratieff

2

THE LONG WAVES IN ECONOMIC LIFE*
By Nikolai D. Kondratieff‖

Foreword

The editors of the Review of Economic Statistics are happy to be able to present in translation the peculiarly important article by Professor Kondratieff, which, under the title "Die langen Wellen der Konjunktur," appeared in the *Archiv für Sozialwissenschaft und Sozialpolitik* in 1926 (vol. 56, no. 3, pp. 573–609). The combining circumstances of an increasing interest in "long waves" and the difficulty of securing access to the original article would alone justify translation and publication of Kondratieff's contribution to the theory of the trade cycle. In addition, the editors would take this means of indicating their intention from time to time of rendering available to the English-using world outstanding articles in foreign periodicals.

This translation of Professor Kondratieff's article was made by Mr. W. F. Stolper of Harvard University. Due to the limitations of space, the editors have taken the liberty to summarize certain sections of this translation. With the exception of a ten-page appendix of tabular material, however, all tables and charts have been included.

I. Introduction

The idea that the dynamics of economic life in the capitalistic social order is not of a simple and linear but rather of a complex and cyclical character is nowadays generally recognized. Science, however, has fallen far short of clarifying the nature and the types of these cyclical, wave-like movements.

When in economics we speak of cycles, we generally mean seven to eleven year business cycles. But these seven to eleven year movements are obviously not the only type of economic cycles.

---

* *The Review of Economic Statistics*, Volume XVII, Number 6, November 1935, pages 105–115. Reprinted by the courtesy of The Review of Economic Statistics.

‖ Formerly Business Research Institute, Moscow.

The dynamics of economic life is in reality more complicated. In addition to the above-mentioned cycles, which we shall agree to call "intermediate," the existence of still shorter waves of about three and one-half years' length has recently been shown to be probable.[1]

But that is not all. There is, indeed, reason to assume the existence of long waves of an average length of about 50 years in the capitalistic economy, a fact which still further complicates the problem of economic dynamics.

II–III. Method

[Sections II and III of Kondratieff's exposition may be summarized as follows:.

The succeeding study is to be confined solely to an inquiry into various problems connected with these long waves. Investigation here is made difficult by the fact that a very long period of observation is presupposed. We have, however, no data before the end of the eighteenth century and even the data that we do have are too scanty and not entirely reliable. Since the material relating to England and France is the most complete, it has formed the chief basis of this inquiry. The statistical methods used were simple when no secular trend was present in the series. If the series displayed a secular trend, as was the case among physical series, the first step was to divide the annual figures by the population, whenever this was logically possible, in order to allow for changes in territory. Then the secular trend was eliminated by the usual statistical methods applied to each series as a whole; and Kondratieff refers specifically to the methods presented by Dr. Warren M. Persons in this REVIEW in 1919 and 1920. The deviations from the secular trend were then smoothed by a nine-year moving average, in order to eliminate the seven to eleven year business cycles, the short cycles, and random fluctuations possibly present.]

---

[1] Cf. J. Kitchin, "Cycles and Trends in Economic Factors," REVIEW OF ECONOMIC STATISTICS [hereafter referred to as "this REVIEW"], v (1923), pp. 10–16.

IV. THE WHOLESALE PRICE LEVEL

While the index of French prices goes back only to the end of the 1850's, the English and American indices date back to the close of the eighteenth century. In order not to overburden this study with figures, the statistical data are presented exclusively in the form of charts.[1]

The index numbers of prices plotted on Chart 1 have been neither smoothed nor treated in any other way. Nevertheless, a mere glance at the chart shows that the price level, despite all deviations and irregularities, exhibits a succession of long waves.

The upswing of the first long wave embraces the period from 1789 to 1814, i.e., 25$\frac{3}{4}$ years; its decline begins in 1814 and ends in 1849, a period of 35 years. The cycle is, therefore, completed in 60 years.[2]

The rise of the second wave begins in 1849 and ends in 1873, lasting 24 years. The turning point, however, is not the same in the United States as in England and France; in the United States the peak occurs in the year 1866, but this is to be explained by the Civil War and casts no doubt on the unity of the picture which the course of the wave exhibits in the two continents. The decline of the second wave begins in 1873 and ends in 1896, a period of 23 years. The length of the second wave is 47 years.

The upward movement of the third wave begins in 1896 and ends in 1920, its duration being 24 years. The decline of the wave, according to all data, begins in 1920.

It is easily seen that the French prices, after the close of the 1850's move generally parallel to the English and American prices.

---

[1] [Ten pages of tabular material were given by Kondratieff at the end of his article. The charts presented in this translation are not merely reproductions of those in the original article but have been drawn anew from the data given in his tabular appendix. A few slight discrepancies between the new charts and those of Kondratieff were discovered, but in no case were the discrepancies significant.—Editors.]

[2] In the upswing, the English index exhibits several peaks, which fall in the years 1799, 1805, 1810, and 1814; but since after the year 1814 a distinctly downward tendency can be observed, we regard this year as the turning point.

CHART 1.—INDEX NUMBERS OF COMMODITY PRICES*
(1901–10 = 100)

France
England
United States
380
360
340
320
300
280
260
240
220
200
180
160
140
120
100
80
60
1780 '85 1790 '95 1800 '05 1810 '15 1820 '25 1830 '35 1840 '45 1850 '55 1860 '65 1870 '75 1880 '85 1890 '95 1900 '05 1910 '15 1920 '25

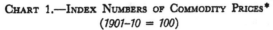

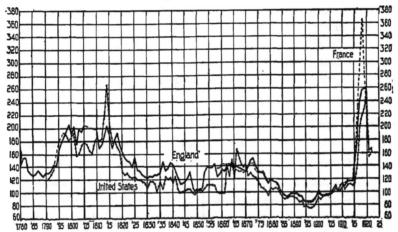

* The *French* data are taken from the *Annuaire Statistique* [Statistique Générale de la France], 1922, p. 341; the index number has been recalculated on a gold basis through use of dollar-franc exchange rates.

For *England*, there is for 1782–1865 the index of Jevons; for 1779–1850, a new index number, computed by Silberling and published in this REVIEW, v (1923); for the period after 1846, we have Sauerbeck's index, which at present is carried on by the *Statist*. Since Silberling's index is based upon more complete data of the prices of individual commodities than that of Jevons, we have used the former for the period 1780–1846. From 1846 on we use Sauerbeck's index number. Both indices have been tied together on the basis of their relation during 1846–50, for which period they are both available; after this procedure, we have shifted the series to a new base, 1901–10. For the period 1801–20 and since 1914, in which periods England was on a paper standard, the index numbers have been recalculated on a gold basis.

For the *United States*, we use the following series, which have been tied together: for 1791–1801, H. V. Roelse (*Quarterly Publications of the American Statistical Association*, December, 1917); 1801–25, A. H. Hansen (*ibid.*, December, 1915); 1825–39, C. H. Juergens (*ibid.*, June, 1911); 1840–90, Falkner (Report from the Committee on Finance of the United States Senate on *Wholesale Prices, Wages, and Transportation*, 52d Congress, 2d session, Report No. 1394, Part 1 [Washington: Government Printing Office, March 3, 1893]); since 1890, the B. L. S. index. All index numbers are on the base 1901–10. For the Greenback period (1862–78), they have been recalculated on a gold basis. All data [except Silberling's index] are taken from the *Annuaire Statistique*, 1922 [which utilizes the sources above cited].

It is, therefore, very probable that this parallelism existed in the preceding period as well.

We conclude, therefore, that three great cycles are present in the movement of the price level during the period since the end of the 1780's, the last of which is only half completed. The waves are not of exactly the same length, their duration varying between 47 and 60 years. The first wave is the longest.

V. The Rate of Interest

The course of the interest rate can be seen most conveniently from the movement of the discount rate and the quotations of

Chart 2.—Quotations of Interest-bearing Securities

+20
+10
0
-10
-20
French rente
English consols
'15 1820 '25 1830 '35 1840 '45 1850 '55 1860 '65 1870 '75 1880 '85 1890 '95 1900 '05 1910 '15 1920 '25

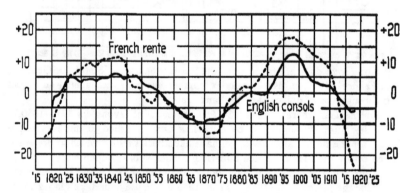

interest-bearing securities. Because the latter depend less on random fluctuations and reflect more accurately the influence of long-run factors, we use here only the quotations of state bonds.

Chart 2 shows the quotations of the French Rente[1] and of English consols.[2] Both have a secular trend during the period of

[1] Until 1825 the quotations of the five-per-cent Rente, after this the quotations of the three-per-cent Rente. In order to connect both series, we have first computed relatives with the base 1825–30 for both series. Then we shifted the base of the combined series to 1901–10, in order to make them comparable with the price curve. The original data are taken from the *Annuaire Statistique* [Statistique Générale de la France], 1922.

[2] According to the data in William Page, ed., *Commerce and Industry*, Vol. 2 (London, 1919), statistical tables, pp. 224–25. Relatives have been calculated from the figures, with the base 1901–10.

observation. The chart shows the deviations from the secular trend smoothed by means of a nine-year moving average.

The quotations of interest-bearing securities manifest, as is well known, a movement opposite to that of general business activity and of the interest rate. Therefore, if long waves are operative in the fluctuations of the interest rate, the movement of bond quotations must run in a direction counter to that of commodity prices. Just this is shown in our chart, which exhibits clearly the long waves in the movement of the quotations and consequently of the interest rate.

The chart starts only after the Napoleonic Wars, i.e., about the time that the first long wave of commodity prices had reached its peak; it does not cover the period of the upswing of the latter. Considering the data at hand, however, we may suppose that the quotations of state bonds took part in this movement also.

English consols actually manifest a decidedly downward tendency between 1792 and 1813. Their quotation in 1792 is 90.04; in 1813, on the other hand, it is 58.81. Although they drop most rapidly in the years 1797 and 1798, yet this steep decline is only an episode, and the general downward tendency from 1792 to 1813 stands out quite clearly.[1]

Accordingly, the period from the beginning of the 1790's up to 1813 appears to be the phase of rising interest rates. This period agrees perfectly with that of the rising wave of commodity prices.

The wave of bond quotations rises after 1813[2]—or the wave of the interest rate declines—even till the middle of the forties. (See the chart.) According to the unsmoothed data, consols reached their peak in 1844; the Rente, in 1845. With this, the first great cycle in the movement of the interest rate is completed.

The downward movement of bond quotations (or the rise of the interest rate) during the second cycle lasts from 1844–45 to

---

[1] Cf. N. J. Silberling, "British Financial Experience, 1790–1830," this REVIEW 1 (1919), p. 289.

[2] The first years have disappeared from our chart because of the use of the nine-year moving average.

1870–74.[1] From this time onward until 1897, the market price of interest-bearing securities rises again, and consequently the interest rate goes down. With this, the second great cycle is completed.

The new decline of the quotations (rise in the rate of interest) lasts from 1897 to 1921. Thus the existence of great cycles in the movement of the interest rate appears very clearly.[2] The periods of these cycles agree rather closely with the corresponding periods in the movement of wholesale commodity prices.

VI–VII. Wages and Foreign Trade

[In Section VI, Kondratieff examines the course of weekly wages of workers in the English cotton-textile industry since 1806 and of English agricultural laborers since 1789.[3] The original wage data are reduced to a gold basis and then expressed in the form of index numbers with 1892 as the base year. Chart 3 presents these wage figures as deviations from trend, smoothed by use

---

[1] According to the original data, consols actually reach their lowest point in 1866, but the general tendency continues to be one of decline until 1874. The slump of quotations in 1866 is connected with the increase in the interest rate just preceding the money-market crisis of that year, and with the Austro-Prussian War.

[2] The existence of these cycles is also confirmed by several other studies: P. Wallich, "Beiträge zur Geschichte des Zinsfusses von 1800 bis zur Gegenwart," *Jahrbücher für Nationalökonomie und Statistik*, III. Folge, Vol. 42, pp. 289–312; J. Lescure, "Hausses et Baisses Générales des Prix," *Revue d'Economie Politique*, Nr. 4 (1912); R. A. Macdonald, "The Rate of Interest Since 1844," *Journal of the Royal Statistical Society*, LXXV (1912), pp. 361–79; T. T. Williams, "The Rate of Discount and the Price of Consols," *ibid.*, pp. 380–400. Also, *ibid.*, pp. 401–11, the discussion of the last-mentioned studies, especially the speech of E. L. Hartley, pp. 404–06.

[3] [Earnings of cotton-textile workers for 1806–1906 are taken from G. H. Wood, *The History of Wages in the Cotton Trade* (London, 1910), p. 127; beginning with 1906, they are from the *Abstract of Labour Statistics*.

For agricultural laborers, wage data for 1789–1896 are from A. L. Bowley, "The Statistics of Wages in the United Kingdom During the Last Hundred Years: Part IV, Agricultural Wages," *Journal of the Royal Statistical Society*, LXII (1899), pp. 555 ff. Thereafter, the figures are from Page, *op. cit.* The data refer to England and Wales.]

of a nine-year moving average. Kondratieff devotes the remainder of this section to a description of the series presented in Chart 3, from which analysis he concludes that, despite the scantiness of the available data, "long waves are undoubtedly present in the movement of wages, the periods of which correspond fairly well with those in commodity prices and the interest rate."

CHART 3.—WAGES IN ENGLAND

Scale For I
Scale for 2
+30
+20
+10
0
-10
+15.0
+10.0
+5.0
0
-5.0
I Agricultural laborers
2-Cotton-textile workers
1790 '95 1800 '05 1810 '15 1820 '25 1830 '35 1840 '45 1850 '55 1860 '65 1870 '75 1880 '85 1890 '95 1900 '05 1910

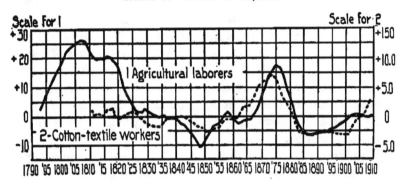

CHART 4.—FRENCH FOREIGN TRADE

+40
+20
0
-20
-40
-60
1830 '35 1840 '45 1850 '55 1860 '65 1870 '75 1880 '85 1890 '95 1900 '05 1910

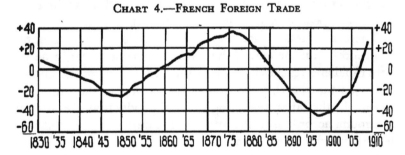

For his foreign-trade series presented in Section VII, Kondratieff takes the sum of French exports and imports. The figures were first corrected for population changes, and thereafter the secular trend (in the form of a second-degree parabola) was eliminated. The resulting deviations, smoothed by use of a nine-year moving average, are presented in Chart 4. After an examination of the chart, the author concludes that the data on foreign trade also show the existence of two great cycles, the periods of which coincide with those observed in the other data.]

VIII. THE PRODUCTION AND CONSUMPTION OF COAL AND PIG IRON, AND THE PRODUCTION OF LEAD

So far we have examined the movements only of such magnitudes, sensitive to changes in business conditions, as possess either a purely value character, e.g., commodity prices, interest rates, and wages, or at least a mixed character such as the data on foreign trade. Our study, however, would lose much of its force if we did not also analyze the behavior of purely physical series.

For this purpose we choose English coal production,[1] and French consumption of coal,[2] as well as the English production of pig iron and of lead.[3] We divided the original figures by the population, and eliminated from the resulting series the secular trends. The deviations from the lines of trend, after being smoothed by use of a nine-year moving average, were then analyzed. The results are shown in Chart 5.

Continuous data are available, unfortunately, only for the period after the 1830's, in part even only after the 1850's. Consequently, only one and one-half to two great cycles can be shown, but these appear with striking clarity in both charts.

There is a retardation in the increase of coal consumption [in France] until the end of the 1840's, then the advance becomes more rapid and reaches its peak in 1865, according to the smoothed curve (on the chart), and in 1873, according to the unsmoothed curve. In the latter year, English coal production also reaches a maximum, according to the unsmoothed curve. Then follows the decline, which comes to an end in 1890–94, giving way to a new long upswing. So we observe in the data relative to the rapidity in the increase of coal production and coal consumption nearly the whole of two large cycles, the periods of which correspond closely to the periods we have already found when considering other series.

Similarly, English production of pig iron and lead indicates sufficiently clearly the existence of one and one-half large cycles.

---

[1] According to the data of W. Page, *op. cit.*

[2] *Annuaire Statistique*, 1908 and 1922.

[3] According to *British and Foreign Trade and Industry*, and the *Statistical Abstract* [*for the United Kingdom*].

CHART 5.—CONSUMPTION OF COAL IN FRANCE AND PRODUCTION OF COAL, PIG IRON AND LEAD IN ENGLAND

Coal production and coal consumption
Scale for France
Scale for England
+40
+20
0
-20
-40
-60
+200
+100
0
-100
-200
-300
Coal consumption
France
Coal production
England
1830 '35 1840 '45 1850 '55 1860 '65 1870 '75 1880 '85 1890 '95 1900 '05 1910 '15

Pig iron and lead production in England
Scale for pig iron
Scale for lead
+20
+10
0
-10
-20
-30
+300
+150
0
-150
-300
-450
Pig iron
Lead
1840 '45 1850 '55 1860 '65 1870 '75 1880 '85 1890 '95 1900 '05 1910 '15 1920

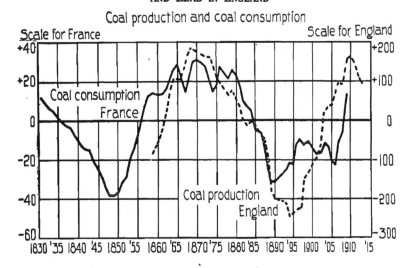

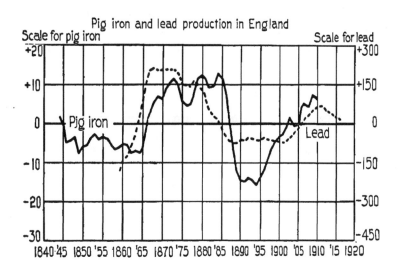

IX. OTHER SERIES

For the sake of brevity, we break off here the systematic analysis of the long waves in the behavior of individual series. We have also examined other data, some of which likewise showed the same periods as those mentioned above, although several other series did not show the cycles with the same clarity. Value series which show long waves are the deposits and the portfolio of the Bank of France, and deposits at the French savings banks; series of a mixed (quantity x price) character are French imports and English imports, and total English foreign trade. As regards the movement of indices of a physical character, the existence of long waves has been established in the coal production of the United States, of Germany, and of the whole world; in the pig-iron production of the United States and of Germany and of the whole world; in the lead and coal production of the United States; in the number of spindles of the cotton industry in the United States; in the cotton acreage in the United States and the oat acreage in France, etc.

It was absolutely impossible, on the other hand, to establish long waves in French cotton consumption; in the wool and sugar production of the United States; and in the movement of several other series.

X. STATISTICAL FINDINGS

The evidence we have presented thus far permits some conclusions.

(1) The movements of the series which we have examined running from the end of the eighteenth century to the present time show long cycles. Although the statistical-mathematical treatment of the series selected is rather complicated, the cycles discovered cannot be regarded as the accidental result of the methods employed. Against such an interpretation is to be set the fact that these waves have been shown with about the same timing in all the more important of the series examined.

(2) In those series which do not exhibit any marked secular trend—e.g., prices—the long cycles appear as a wave-like move-

TABLE 1

Country and series	First cycle		Second cycle		Third cycle	
	Beginning of rise	Beginning of decline	Beginning of rise	Beginning of decline	Beginning of rise	Probable beginning of decline
France						
1. Prices.........................	....	....	....	1873	1896	1920
2. Interest rate................	....	1816*	1844	1872	1894	1921
3. Portfolio of the Bank of France	....	1810*	1851	1873	1902	1914
4. Deposits at the savings banks	....	....	1844	1874	1892	....
5. Wages of coal miners........	....	....	1849	1874	1895	....
6. Imports.....................	....	....	1848	1880	1896	1914
7. Exports.....................	....	....	1848	1872	1894	1914
8. Total foreign trade..........	....	....	1848	1872	1896	1914
9. Coal consumption...........	....	....	1849	1873	1896	1914
10. Oat acreage[1]...............	....	....	1850*	1875	1892	1915
England						
1. Prices.....................	1789	1814	1849	1873	1896	1920
2. Interest rate...............	1790	1816	1844	1874	1897	1921
3. Wages of agricultural laborers	1790	1812–17	1844	1875	1889	....
4. Wages of textile workers.....	....	1810*	1850†	1874	1890	....
5. Foreign trade...............	....	1810*	1842‡	1873	1894	-1914
6. Coal production.............	....	....	1850*	1873	1893	1914
7. Pig iron production.........	....	....	....	1871§	1891	1914
8. Lead production.............	....	....	....	1870	1892	1914
United States						
1. Prices.....................	1790	1814	1849	1866	1896	1920
2. Pig iron production.........	....	....	....	1875–80	1900	1920
3. Coal production.............	....	....	....	1893	1896	1918
4. Cotton acreage..............	....	....	....	1874–81	1892–95	1915
Germany						
Coal production...............	....	....	....	1873‖	1895	1915
Whole world[2]						
1. Pig iron production.........	....	....	....	1872¶	1894	1914
2. Coal production.............	....	....	....	1873	1896	1914

[1] Reversed cycles.
[2] The data which refer to the whole world have not been corrected for population changes.
* Approximate dates.
† Another minimum falls in the year 1835.
‡ Other minima lie in the years 1837 and 1855.
§ Another maximum falls in the year 1881.
‖ Another maximum falls in the year 1883.
¶ Another maximum falls in the year 1882.

ment about the average level. In the series, on the other hand, the movement of which shows such a trend, the cycles accelerate or retard the rate of growth.

(3) In the several series examined, the turning points of the long waves correspond more or less accurately. This is shown clearly by Table 1, which combines the results of the investigation not only of the data considered above but also of several other series.[1]

It is easy to see from this table that there is a very close correspondence in the timing of the wave movements of the series in the individual countries, in spite of the difficulties present in the treatment of these data. Deviations from the general rule that prevails in the sequence of the cycles are very rare. It seems to us that the absence of such exceptions is more remarkable than would be their presence.

(4) Although for the time being we consider it to be impossible to fix exactly upon the years that marked the turning points of the long cycles, and although the method according to which the statistical data have been analyzed permits an error of 5–7 years in the determination of the years of such turnings, the following limits of these cycles can nevertheless be presented as being those most probable:

First long wave
{
1. The rise lasted from the end of the 1780's or beginning of the 1790's until 1810–17.
2. The decline lasted from 1810–17 until 1844–51.

Second long wave
{
1. The rise lasted from 1844–51 until 1870–75.
2. The decline lasted from 1870–75 until 1890–96.

Third long wave
{
1. The rise lasted from 1890–96 until 1914–20.
2. The decline probably begins in the years 1914–20.

(5) Naturally, the fact that the movement of the series examined runs in long cycles does not yet prove that such cycles also

---

[1] Table 1 enumerates the maxima and minima according to the original data. The problem of the most accurate method for the determination of the maxima and minima would deserve a special analysis; at present we leave this question open. We believe only that the indicated turning points are the most probable ones.

dominate the movement of all other series. A later examination with this point especially in mind will have to be made to show which ones of these share the described wave-like movement. As already pointed out, our investigation has also extended to series in which no such waves were evident. On the other hand, it is by no means essential that the long waves embrace all series.

(6) The long waves that we have established above relative to the series most important in economic life are international; and the timing of these cycles corresponds fairly well for European capitalistic countries. On the basis of the data that we have adduced, we can venture the statement that the same timing holds also for the United States. The dynamics in the development of capitalism, however, and especially the timing of the fluctuations in the latter country may have peculiarities.

XI. Empirical Characteristics

We were led to these conclusions by the study of statistical series characterizing the movement of the capitalist economy. From another point of view, the historical material relating to the development of economic and social life as a whole confirms the hypothesis of long waves. We neither can nor shall undertake here an analysis of this material. Nevertheless, several general propositions which we have arrived at concerning the existence and importance of long waves may be presented.

(1) The long waves belong really to the same complex dynamic process in which the intermediate cycles of the capitalistic economy with their principal phases of upswing and depression run their course. These intermediate cycles, however, secure a certain stamp from the very existence of the long waves. Our investigation demonstrates that during the rise of the long waves, years of prosperity are more numerous, whereas years of depression predominate during the downswing.[1]

(2) During the recession of the long waves, agriculture, as a rule, suffers an especially pronounced and long depression. This

---

[1] Cf. A. Spiethoff, "Krisen," (*Handwörterbuch der Staatswissenschaften*, 4th edition).

was what happened after the Napoleonic Wars; it happened again from the beginning of the 1870's onward; and the same can be observed in the years after the World War.[1]

(3) During the recession of the long waves, an especially large number of important discoveries and inventions in the technique of production and communication are made, which, however, are usually applied on a large scale only at the beginning of the next long upswing.

(4) At the beginning of a long upswing, gold production increases as a rule, and the world market [for goods] is generally enlarged by the assimilation of new and especially of colonial countries.

(5) It is during the period of the rise of the long waves, i.e., during the period of high tension in the expansion of economic forces, that, as a rule, the most disastrous and extensive wars and revolutions occur.

It is to be emphasized that we attribute to these recurring relationships an empirical character only, and that we do not by any means hold that they contain the explanation of the long waves.

XII. The Nature of Long Waves

Is it possible to maintain that the existence of long cycles in the dynamics of the capitalist economy is proved on the basis of the preceding statements? The relevant data which we were able to quote cover about 140 years. This period comprises two and one-half cycles only. Although the period embraced by the data is sufficient to decide the question of the existence of long waves, it is not enough to enable us to assert beyond doubt the cyclical character of those waves. Nevertheless we believe that the available data are sufficient to declare this cyclical character to be very probable.

We are led to this conclusion not only by the consideration of the factual material, but also because the objections to the assumption of long cyclical waves are very weak.

---

[1] Cf. Ernle, *English Farming Past and Present* (London, 1922), and G. F. Warren and F. A. Pearson, *The Agricultural Situation* (New York, 1924).

It has been objected that long waves lack the regularity which business cycles display.   But this is wrong.   If one defines "regularity" as repetition in regular time-intervals, then long waves possess this characteristic as much as the intermediate ones.   A strict periodicity in social and economic phenomena does not exist at all—neither in the long nor in the intermediate waves.   The length of the latter fluctuates at least between 7 and 11 years, i.e., 57 per cent.   The length of the long cycles fluctuates between 48 and 60 years, i.e., 25 per cent only.

If regularity is understood to be the similarity and simultaneity of the fluctuations of different series, then it is present to the same degree in the long as in the intermediate waves.

If, finally, regularity is understood to consist in the fact that the intermediate waves are an international phenomenon, then the long waves do not differ from the latter in this respect either.

Consequently, there is no less regularity in the long waves than in the intermediate ones, and if we want to designate the latter as cyclical, we are bound not to deny this characterization to the former.

It has been pointed out [by other critics] that the long waves— as distinct from the intermediate ones which come from causes within the capitalistic system—are conditioned by casual, extra-economic circumstances and events, such as (1) changes in technique, (2) wars and revolutions, (3) the assimilation of new countries into the world economy, and (4) fluctuations in gold production.

These considerations are important.   But they, too, are not valid.   Their weakness lies in the fact that they reverse the causal connections and take the consequence to be the cause, or see an accident where we have really to deal with a law governing the events.   In the preceding paragraphs, we have deliberately, though briefly, considered the establishment of some empirical rules for the movement of long waves.   These regularities help us now to evaluate correctly the objections just mentioned.

1. *Changes in technique* have without doubt a very potent influence on the course of capitalistic development.   But nobody has proved them to have an accidental and external origin.

Changes in the technique of production presume (1) that the relevant scientific-technical discoveries and inventions have been made, and (2) that it is *economically* possible to use them. It would be an obvious mistake to deny the creative element in scientific-technical discoveries and inventions. But from an objective viewpoint, a still greater error would occur if one believed that the direction and intensity of those discoveries and inventions were entirely accidental; it is much more probable that such direction and intensity are a function of the necessities of real life and of the preceding development of science and technique.[1]

Scientific-technical inventions in themselves, however, are insufficient to bring about a real change in the technique of production. They can remain ineffective so long as economic conditions favorable to their application are absent. This is shown by the example of the scientific-technical inventions of the seventeenth and eighteenth centuries which were used on a large scale only during the industrial revolution at the close of the eighteenth century. If this be true, then the assumption that changes in technique are of a random character and do not in fact spring from economic necessities loses much of its weight. We have seen before that the development of technique itself is part of the rhythm of the long waves.

2. *Wars and revolutions* also influence the course of economic development very strongly. But wars and revolutions do not come out of a clear sky, and they are not caused by arbitrary acts of individual personalities. They originate from real, especially economic, circumstances. The assumption that wars and revolutions acting from the outside cause long waves evokes the question as to

---

[1] One of the best and most compelling arguments for the assumption that scientific and technical inventions and discoveries are not made accidentally but are intimately connected with the needs of practical life is given by the numerous cases in which the same inventions and discoveries are made at the same time at different places and entirely independently of one another. Cf. the long list of such cases in W. F. Ogburn, *Social Change* (New York, 1924), p. 90. Cf. also Dannemann, *Die Naturwissenschaften in ihrer Entwickelung und in ihrem Zusammenhange* (Leipzig, 1923).

why they themselves follow each other with regularity and solely during the upswing of long waves. Much more probable is the assumption that wars originate in the acceleration of the pace and the increased tension of economic life, in the heightened economic struggle for markets and raw materials, and that social shocks happen most easily under the pressure of new economic forces.

Wars and revolutions, therefore, can also be fitted into the rhythm of the long waves and do not prove to be the forces from which these movements originate, but rather to be one of their symptoms. But once they have occurred, they naturally exercise a potent influence on the pace and direction of economic dynamics.

3. As regards the *opening-up of new countries for the world economy*, it seems to be quite obvious that this cannot be considered an outside factor which will satisfactorily explain the origin of long waves. The United States have been known for a relatively very long time; for some reason or other they begin to be entangled in the world economy on a major scale only from the middle of the nineteenth century. Likewise, the Argentine and Canada, Australia and New Zealand, were discovered long before the end of the nineteenth century, although they begin to be entwined in the world economy to a significant extent only with the coming of the 1890's. It is perfectly clear historically that, in the capitalistic economic system, new regions are opened for commerce during those periods in which the desire of old countries for new markets and new sources of raw materials becomes more urgent than theretofore. It is equally apparent that the limits of this expansion of the world economy are determined by the degree of this urgency. If this be true, then the opening of new countries does not provoke the upswing of a long wave. On the contrary, a new upswing makes the exploitation of new countries, new markets, and new sources of raw materials necessary and possible, in that it accelerates the pace of capitalistic economic development.

4. There remains the question whether the *discovery of new gold mines*, the *increase in gold production*, and a consequent *increase in the gold stock* can be regarded as a casual, outside factor causing the long waves.

An increase in gold production leads ultimately to a rise in prices and to a quickening in the tempo of economic life. But this does not mean that the changes in gold production are of a casual, outside character and that the waves in prices and in economic life are likewise caused by chance. We consider this to be not only unproved but positively wrong. This contention originates from the belief, first, that the discovery of gold mines and the perfection of the technique of gold production are accidental and, secondly, that every discovery of new gold mines and of technical inventions in the sphere of gold production brings about an increase in the latter. However great may be the creative element in these technical inventions and the significance of chance in these discoveries, yet they are not entirely accidental. Still less accidental—and this is the main point—are the fluctuations in gold production itself. These fluctuations are by no means simply a function of the activity of inventors and of the discoveries of new gold mines. On the contrary, the intensity of inventors' and explorers' activity and the application of technical improvement in the sphere of gold production, as well as the resulting increase of the latter, depend upon other, more general causes. The dependence of gold production upon technical inventions and discoveries of new gold mines is only secondary and derived.

Although gold is a generally recognized embodiment of value and, therefore, is generally desired, it is only a commodity. And like every commodity it has a cost of production. But if this be true, then gold production—even in newly discovered mines—can increase significantly only if it becomes more profitable, i.e., if the relation of the value of the gold itself to its cost of production (and this is ultimately the prices of other commodities) becomes more favorable. If this relation is unfavorable, even gold mines the richness of which is by no means yet exhausted may be shut down; if it is favorable, on the other hand, even relatively poor mines will be exploited.

When is the relation of the value of gold to that of other commodities most favorable for gold production? We know that commodity prices reach their lowest level toward the end of a long wave. This means that at this time gold has its highest purchasing power, and gold production becomes most favorable. This can be illustrated by the figures in Table 2.

Gold production, as can be seen from these figures, becomes more profitable as we approach a low point in the price level and a high point in the purchasing power of gold (1895 and the following years).

TABLE 2.—SELECTED STATISTICS OF GOLD MINING IN THE TRANSVAAL, 1890–1913*

Year	Cost of production	Profit
	Per ton of gold ore	
1890....................................	42 *sh.* 2 *d.*	7 *sh.* 2 *d.*
1895....................................	33 *sh.* 5 *d.*	11 *sh.* 11 *d.*
1899....................................	28 *sh.* 0 *d.*	14 *sh.* 3 *d.*
1903....................................	24 *sh.* 9 *d.*	14 *sh.* 11 *d.*
1906....................................	22 *sh.* 2 *d.*	11 *sh.* 6 *d.*
1913....................................	17 *sh.* 11 *d.*	9 *sh.* 10 *d.*

* Cf. W. A. Berridge, "The World's Gold Supply," this REVIEW, 11 (1920), p. 184.

It is clear, furthermore, that the stimulus to increased gold production necessarily becomes stronger the further a long wave declines. We, therefore, can suppose theoretically that gold production must in general increase most markedly when the wave falls most sharply, and vice versa.

In reality, however, the connection is not as simple as this but becomes more complicated, mainly just because of the effect of the changes in the technique of gold production and the discovery of new mines. It seems to us, indeed, that even improvements in technique and new gold discoveries obey the same fundamental law as does gold production itself, with more or less regularity in timing. Improvements in the technique of gold production and the discovery of new gold mines actually do bring about a lowering in the cost of production of gold; they influence the relation of these costs to the value of gold, and consequently the extent of gold production.   But then it is obvious that exactly at the time when the relation of the value of gold to its cost becomes more unfavorable than theretofore, the need for technical improvements in gold mining and for the discovery of new mines necessarily becomes more urgent and thus stimulates research in this field.   There is, of course, a time-lag, until this urgent necessity, though already recognized, leads to positive success.   In reality, therefore, gold discoveries and technical improvements in gold mining will reach their peak only when the long wave has already passed its peak, i.e., perhaps in the middle of the downswing.   The available facts confirm this supposition.[1]   In the period after the 1870's, the following gold discoveries were made: 1881 in Alaska, 1884 in the Transvaal, 1887 in West Australia, 1890 in Colorado, 1894 in Mexico, 1896 in the Klondike.   The inventions in the field of gold-mining technique, and especially the most important ones of this period (the inventions for the treatment of ore), were also made during the 1880's, as is well known.

Gold discoveries and technical improvements, if they occur, will naturally influence gold production.   They can have the effect that the increase in gold production takes place somewhat earlier than at the end of the downswing of the long wave.   They also can assist the expansion of gold production, once that limit is reached.   This is precisely what happens in reality.   Especially after the decline in the 1870's, a persistent, though admittedly slender, increase in gold production begins about the year 1883;[2] whereas, in spite of the disturbing influences of discoveries and inventions, the upswing really begins only after gold has reached its greatest purchasing power; and the increased production is due not only to the newly discovered gold fields but in a considerable degree also to the old ones.   This is illustrated by the figures in Table 3.

---

[1] Berridge, *loc. cit.*, p. 181.
[2] Cf. *Statistical Abstract of the United States*, 1922, pp. 708–09.

TABLE 3.—GOLD PRODUCTION, 1890–1900

(*Unit: thousand ounces*)

	World total	Trans-vaal	United States	Aus-tralia	Russia	Canada	Mexico	India
1890......	5,749	440	1,589	1,588	1,135	65	737	9
1895......	9,615	2,017	2,255	2,356	1,388	101	290	230
1900......	14,838	3,638	3,437	4,461	1,072	1,029	411	412

Source: Berridge, *loc. cit.*, p. 182.

From the foregoing one may conclude, it seems to us, that gold production, even though its increase can be a condition for an advance in commodity prices and for a general upswing in economic activity, is yet subordinate to the rhythm of the long waves and consequently cannot be regarded as a causal and random factor that brings about these movements from the outside.

XIII. CONCLUSIONS

The objections to the regular cyclical character of the long waves, therefore, seem to us to be unconvincing.

In view of this circumstance and considering also the positive reasons developed above, we think that, *on the basis of the available data, the existence of long waves of cyclical character is very probable.*

At the same time, we believe ourselves justified in saying that the long waves, if existent at all, are a very important and essential factor in economic development, a factor the effects of which can be found in all the principal fields of social and economic life.

Even granting the existence of long waves, one is, of course, not justified in believing that economic dynamics consists only in fluctuations around a certain level. The course of economic activity represents beyond doubt a process of development, but this development obviously proceeds not only through intermediate waves but also through long ones. The problem of economic development *in toto* cannot be discussed here.

In asserting the existence of long waves and in denying that they arise out of random causes, we are also of the opinion that the long waves arise out of causes which are inherent in the essence of the capitalistic economy. This naturally leads to the question as to the nature of these causes. We are fully aware of the difficulty and great importance of this question; but in the preceding sketch we had no intention of laying the foundations for an appropriate theory of long waves.[1]

---

[1] I arrived at the hypothesis concerning the existence of long waves in the years 1919–21. Without going into a special analysis, I formulated my general thesis for the first time shortly thereafter in my study, *The World Economy and Economic Fluctuations in the War and Post-War Period* (*Mirovoje chozjajstvo i jego konjunktury vo vremja i posle vojny* [Moscow, 1922]). During the winter and spring of 1925, I wrote a special study on "Long Waves in Economic Life" ("Bol'schije cykly konjunktury"), which was published in the volume of the Institute for Business Cycle Research, *Problems of Economic Fluctuations* (*Voprosy konjunktury*, Vol. 1). Only at the beginning of 1926 did I become acquainted with S. de Wolff's article "Prosperitäts- und Depressionsperioden," *Der lebendige Marxismus, Festgabe zum 70. Geburtstage von Karl Kautsky*. De Wolff in many points reaches the same result as I do. The works of J. van Gelderns, which de Wolff cites and which have evidently been published only in Dutch, are unknown to me.

Printed in the USA
CPSIA information can be obtained
at www.ICGtesting.com
LVHW071635020224
770787LV00003B/379